# essential guide to
# cake decorating

This is a Parragon Publishing Book

This edition published in 2006

Parragon Publishing
Queen Street House
4 Queen Street
Bath BA1 1HE, UK



Designed, produced and packaged by
Stonecastle Graphics Limited

Text by Alex Barker
Cake designs by Alex Barker
Photography by Steve Moss
Edited by Bridget Jones
Designed by Sue Pressley and Paul Turner

With special thanks to Lynne A. Strafford for her cakes and cake inspirations and to Kenwood for the loan of the latest Kenwood Major.



ISBN 1-40545-746-5

Printed in China

## Using this book

- The following abbreviations for spoon measures are used throughout: tsp = teaspoon; tbsp = tablespoon. These refer to measuring spoons, not cutlery. All spoon measures are level unless otherwise stated.
  - 1/4tsp = 1.25ml
  - 1/2tsp = 2.5ml
  - 1tsp = 5ml
  - 1tbsp = 15ml
- For best results when making light cakes, use free-range eggs.
- Oven temperatures are for standard appliances. Please check the manufacturer's instructions for your oven, particularly for different types of fan or fan-assisted ovens.
- Use cooking times as a guide: results may vary slightly in different ovens and this may make a difference when baking cakes. It is a good idea to make a note of any slight variations in cooking times in your oven for optimum results.
- Recipes using raw or lightly cooked eggs should be avoided by infants, the elderly, pregnant women, convalescents, and anyone suffering from an illness. If you make cakes for gifts or for public occasions or are worried about the use of raw egg in marzipan or royal icing, buy dried egg products instead. These ingredients have been heat treated to ensure they are safe. Alternatively, buy marzipan or icing.
- Follow the instructions carefully.
- Safety is very important – children should always be supervised by a responsible adult while in the kitchen. Sharp tools, such as knives and scissors, and small objects, such as icing nozzles which could cause choking if swallowed, should be kept out of the reach of young children.
- The publishers and their agents cannot accept liability for loss, damage or injury however caused.

# essential guide to
# cake decorating

Alex Barker

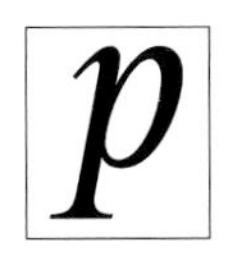

# Contents

# Introduction

**In the 21st Century, teatime often still means 'cake' and even though we rarely make time for tea in the old-fashioned way, most of us will not turn down the occasional offer of a slice of cake. However, turning an everyday cake into a glamorous gâteau or a crazily decorated party piece requires a little more than just baking.**

Cake decorating can be a craft, a hobby or even a business. The skills used at the highest level of sugarcraft require training, practice and expertise. Most of us simply want to enjoy being creative, and taking pride in making something really special or unusual. Making a beautifully decorated cake for someone, or for a family occasion, is a real gift of love and time.

Today's cakes are as simple and stylish, or as colorful and daring as you want them to be. Finding the right design or idea is the first most important stage – frills, ribbons and roses suit some occasions; a brightly colored design with edible caricatures another; or fresh or frosted flowers or fruits may be appropriate. You may well be surprised how easy it is to make a creative cake if you take the time to select and plan a design. Look around at the tools available to turn an idea into reality.

The *Essential Guide to Cake Decorating* describes all you need to know about simple stylish cake decorating, from the basic cake recipes to a range of stunning designs. The first half of the book covers the recipes, techniques and skills that will equip you to make any of the cakes with confidence. Whether you want a Victoria sponge cake, a dark fruit cake or other favorites, like rich chocolate cake or carrot cake, they are all here. Professional tips, guides to quantities for making larger cakes, and information on choosing the right equipment are all included. Learn how to use classic methods for marzipan and royal icing, or soft sugar paste for exciting effects.

The second half of the book leads you carefully, step-by-step, through the stages in making 24 beautiful cakes. It doesn't matter how inexperienced you are, the techniques and guidance in the early pages will show you all you need to know. Discover elegant designs based on surprisingly simple piping; model charming little penguins; or succulent-looking raspberries and bramble berries. Alternatively, try your hand at pretty delicate butterfly run-outs, or stunning bronze cut-out doves. Why not simply have fun with the family, making fabulous cup cakes?

PME
57R
ENGLAND

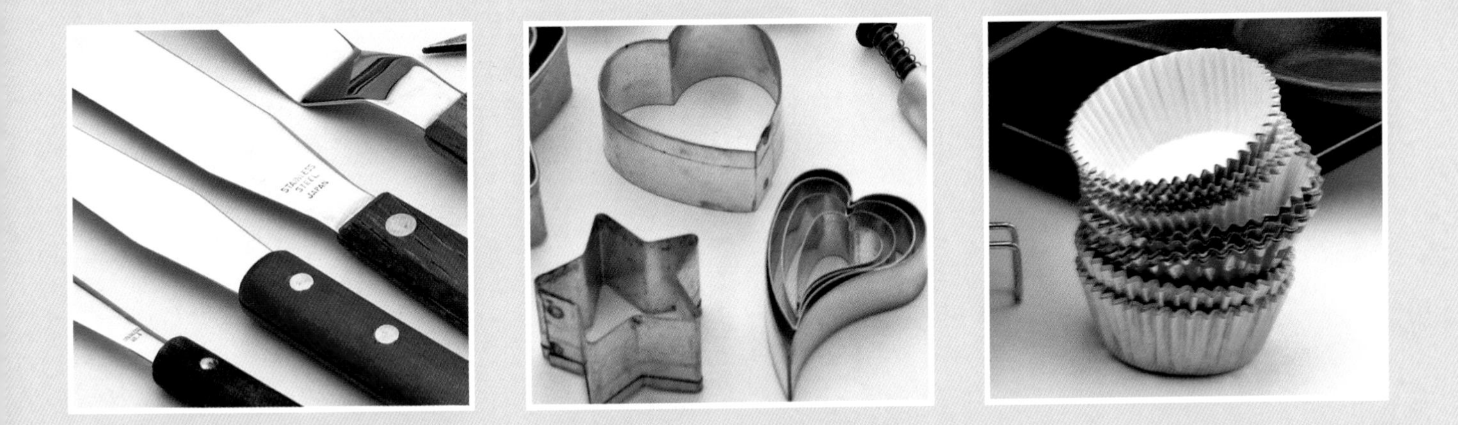

# Planning Perfect Cakes

There is such an array of recipes, designs, equipment, pans, gadgets, ingredients and colors that making the right choice is the first important step. If possible, start with a design outline, then collect everything needed to make and complete the cake. If you have a specialist cake decorating supplier on your doorstep you are lucky; if not, allow plenty of time for mail order delivery of any special cutters, colors or cake boards required.

As well as a reliable recipe, turning out a great basic cake demands a good pan, prepared properly, and an oven that cooks evenly and steadily at the right temperature. Generally, there's no need to buy a new pan if you already have one of the correct size and shape – simply take care to line it properly. Pans of unusual shape or size are available to hire from catering shops or specialist cake suppliers. Make a point of keeping all your cake-decorating tools stored safely together, for example in a toolbox. Many items are tiny, easily lost and costly to replace.

# Baking Equipment

**Most cooks already have a selection of baking equipment, often handed down through generations, and few have to buy everything from new. However, using the right item for the job does make all the difference, especially when it comes to baking pans and mixers.**

- **Boards:** If possible use separate boards for general cooking and making sugar decorations. Small white (or colored) smooth plastic boards are available from specialist cake decorating shops.
- **Brushes:** Use a variety of sizes for greasing pans, brushing on apricot glaze, moistening surfaces with water or lemon juice, and painting fine designs.
- **Cake boards:** Available in many sizes and shapes, thin or thick, in both gold and silver.
- **Cake pans:** Available in all sizes and shapes. Choose good-quality non-stick pans with loose bases. Keep your pans really clean and dry. Hire unusual shapes or large sizes for special occasions.
- **Cooling racks:** Cool cakes and bakes on wire racks.
- **Knives:** Palette knives, both large and small, are important for spreading, smoothing and flattening. You will also need a selection of good, sharp cook's knives for cutting and trimming cakes.
- **Mixers:** If you frequently make cakes you will find a good mixer indispensable. An electric hand-held mixer is the most economical and useful for creaming light mixtures, whisking eggs, or whipping cream. A large free-standing food mixer with beater and whisk is ideal for frostings, royal icing, and fruit cakes. Food processors are not ideal for cakes, or frostings unless they have a whisk blade and a slow speed setting for gentle mixing.
- **Papers and wraps:** You will need wax paper and non-stick baking parchment to line pans, draw designs or make piping bags. Plastic wrap keeps frosting and marzipan soft and airtight. Foil is a good base on which to set chocolate and caramel designs. Paper towel can be used to support shapes and dry items.
- **Sieves:** For sifting flour and sugar; also for finely dredging cakes with confectioners' sugar or cocoa powder (unsweetened).
- **String:** To tie paper around cake pans when baking rich fruit cakes, to protect them from over cooking on the outside; also useful for measuring pans or cakes of awkward shapes.

**Pictures left, from top:**

- *Use brushes to keep surfaces clean, grease pans or paint decorations. Tweezers and craft knives allow pin-point precision on fine cakes.*
- *Keep cutting knives sharp. Have a good selection of palette knives to move even the smallest item with care.*
- *Good-quality pans cook evenly and clean easily; cakes will also come out easily.*
- *Cake boards can be used in many ways and can be covered with sugar paste or pretty paper to suit your design.*

*A good mixer will save a lot of hard work.*

# Lining Cake Pans

## Preparing a Round Pan for a Fruit Cake

1 Cut two circles of wax paper for the base and a strip twice the depth and just larger than the circumference of the pan. Fold in half lengthwise and make a 1in fold along one edge of this strip. Make angled cuts into the folded edge.

2 Place one circle in the base of the pan, then line the inside with the strip, cut edge down. Overlap the cut edge to to curve it neatly.

3 Place the second circle of paper in the pan to cover the overlapping cuts around the edge. Lightly grease the base and sides.

4 Tie a band of double-thick brown paper around the outside of the pan. Place the pan on folded newspaper or brown paper on a baking tray.

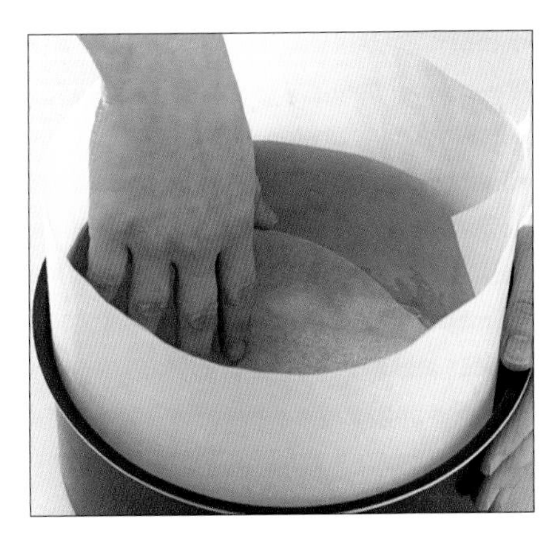

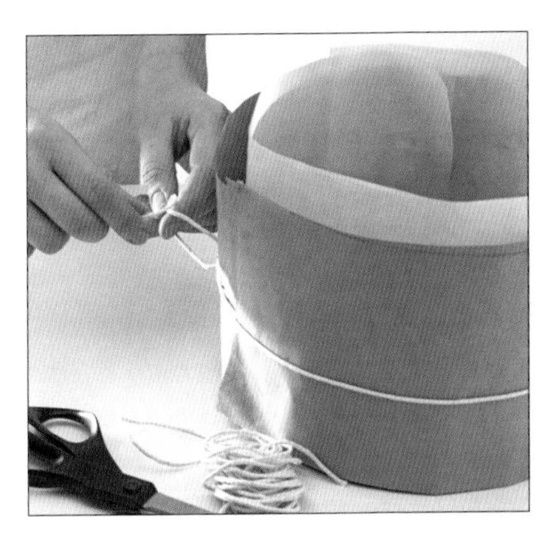

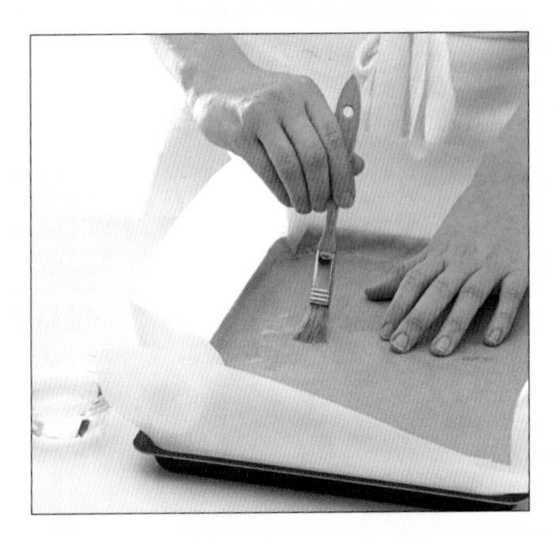

## Lining a Jelly Roll Pan

1 Cut a rectangle of wax paper 2in bigger than the pan on all sides. Place the pan on the paper and cut into the corners so the paper overlaps neatly in the corners.

2 Grease the pan lightly so the paper sticks. Place the paper in the pan, grease lightly and sprinkle with flour. Shake off the excess flour before filling with sponge cake mixture.

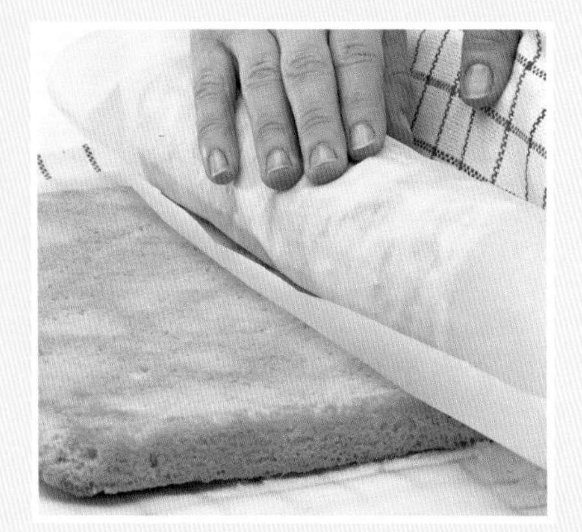

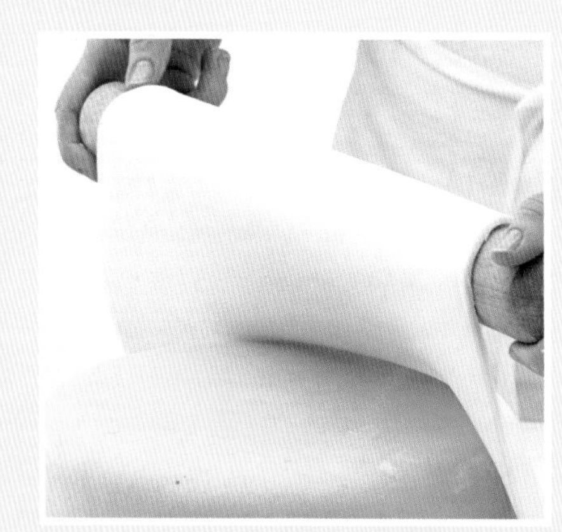

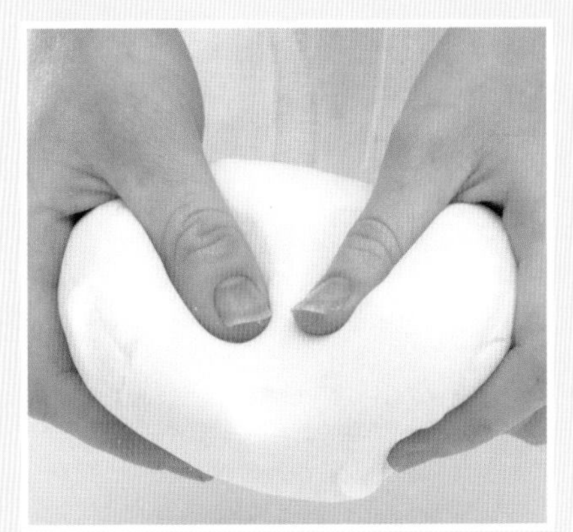

# Recipes for Success

Using the very best ingredients is the base of any good cake. For example, sponge cake especially, benefits from the use of fresh free-range eggs for their rich golden color and light-as-air texture. Fruit cakes benefit from good dried fruit that is full of moist richness. Use good quality vanilla extract – not synthetic flavoring – particularly for delicate sponge cakes in which its distinct warm flavor sings through.

Use equipment wisely: a food mixer can save time and effort but be aware of the potential for over mixing. A light sponge cake needs a light touch for a well-risen springy result. The initial creaming of fat and sugar to a pale fluffy texture helps the ingredients for a fruit cake to mix well. Beating royal icing to a thick glossy cloud can be very tough on your wrists.

Discover the right techniques that result in the perfect finish. Whether you prefer working with classic royal icing or the more immediate, hands-on sugar paste, the following pages have lots of advice and tips to share.

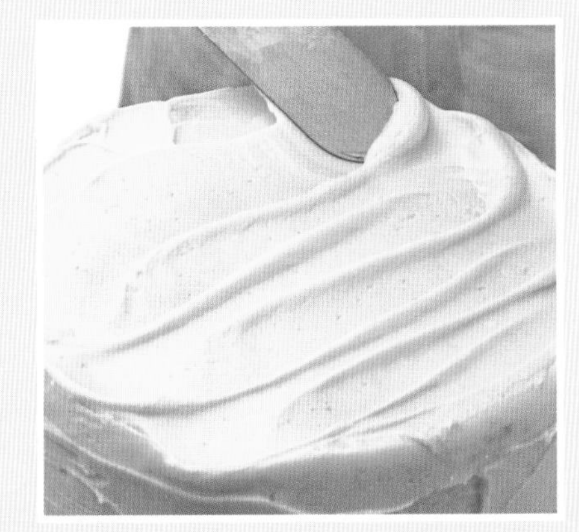

# Simple Sponge Cakes

**Making a good plain sponge cake does not require impossible skill, simply the right recipe and a little time. This cake can then form the base for a wide variety of other cakes, from cup cakes to fruit gâteau, novelty shapes, and elaborately decorated celebration cakes. Cake trimmings can be used in wonderful weekend desserts. A sponge cake is the most versatile cake to have in your repertoire.**

### Sponge cake tips

- To test if a sponge cake is cooked, press gently on the top with your finger tips. If the imprint quickly disappears, the cake is cooked.
- Listen to your sponge cake and if it is still crackling furiously it is not fully cooked!
- For a really light Genoese sponge cake, sift the flour three times to incorporate plenty of air and whisk the eggs over a pan of hot water.
- To freeze a sponge cake, cool thoroughly. Double wrap in plastic wrap and then in foil. Allow 1 hour to thaw, but if cutting into layers do this while still part frozen.
- Using a food processor to make a sponge cake takes a matter of minutes and the only difference is that it will not be quite as light and fluffy as the hand-mixed version. Simply mix everything together in the machine on its slowest speed for as short a time as necessary. When well mixed, spoon into the pans.

### Variations

*quantities for a 3-egg mixture*

- **Lemon or/orange:** Add 2tsp orange flower water, or the finely grated zest of 1/2 lemon or orange with the egg yolks.
- **Chocolate:** Replace 1tbsp flour with sifted unsweetened cocoa powder and add 1-2tsp extra sugar.
- **Nuts:** Replace 1/4 cup flour with 1/4 cup of finely ground almonds or hazelnuts.
- **Coffee:** Dissolve 2tsp instant coffee in 1tsp boiling water and blend in with the eggs.

## Victoria Sponge Cake

**The basic proportions of this cake are well worth remembering so you can whip up this popular family treat at a moment's notice. One hour from start to finish is really all it takes – even less if you use a food processor.**

Serves 4-6

3/4 cup butter or margarine, softened
3/4 cup superfine sugar
3 eggs, lightly beaten with 1-2tsp vanilla extract
1 1/2 cup self-rising flour, sifted

1 Preheat the oven to 180°C/350°F/gas mark 4. Lightly grease the base and sides of one 7in cake pan, or two sandwich pans. Line the base with paper and grease this.

2 Cream the soft butter and sugar in a mixing bowl until pale and fluffy. Gently beat in the eggs and vanilla, gradually adding the flour.

3 When the ingredients are smoothly combined, without too much beating, place the mixture in the pan or divide it evenly between the two pans. Flatten the top or tops with a wetted knife and place in the middle of the oven, on the same shelf if possible, when baking two cakes.

4 Bake for about 20 minutes.The cooked cakes should be light golden, well risen but flat on the top and springy to the touch. Leave to part cool in the pan on a damp cloth for speed and then turn out onto a cooling rack and leave until cold.

**Victoria Sponge Cake Proportions for Pan Sizes (one deep pan or two sandwich pans)**

6in round pan: 1/2 cup fat, 1/2 cup superfine sugar and 1 cup self-rising flour to 2 eggs
7in round pan: 3/4 cup fat, 3/4 cup superfine sugar and 1 1/2 cup self-rising flour to 3 eggs
8in round pan: 1 cup fat, 1 1/4 cup superfine sugar and 2 cups self-rising flour to 4 eggs

### Note

Remember that cooking times may vary depending on the oven used. Cake mixture in one deep pan will take longer to cook than when divided into two pans. Use cooking times as a guide.

## Genoese Sponge Cake

**The Genoese sponge cake (*Genoise* in French) is a whisked sponge cake with a very light open texture. Whisked sponge cakes can be fatless, but a little melted butter is added to a Genoese for a richer result and improved keeping qualities. This type of cake is used for Jelly rolls, ladyfingers, flans and layered gâteau. It is very quick to cook and impressive to serve.**

1 Preheat the oven to 180°C/350°F/gas mark 4. Grease and line one 9in x 14in Jelly roll pan, or two 7in round sponge cake pans.

2 Sift the flour and salt together two or three times for a really light result.

3 Place the eggs and sugar in a large mixing bowl and whisk, with an electric beater, for about 10 minutes or until the mixture is really thick, creamy, and pale. A trail should be left in the mixture when you lift out the beaters.

4 Use a large spatula to fold in the sifted flour and melted butter, carefully and gently folding until smoothly mixed. It is vital to fold in all the flour evenly but try not to overmix as this will reduce the lightness of the cake.

5 Pour into the prepared sponge cake pans and bake for 10-12 minutes, until pale golden, just firm to the touch but very springy. Leave in the pan to cool for 3-5 minutes then transfer to a wire rack.

**Makes one jelly roll or two 7in sponge cakes**

1 cup all-purpose flour, sieved
pinch of salt
3 eggs
1/2 cup superfine sugar
1tbsp melted butter

## Rolling Jelly Roll

1 While the cake is cooking, place a clean dish towel on a flat surface. Cover with wax paper and add a good sprinkling of superfine sugar. Invert the freshly-baked cake carefully onto this. Gently remove the baking paper.

2 Trim any crisp or uneven edges. Make a shallow cut 1in in from the narrow edge of the cake for easy rolling.

3 Cover with a clean sheet of wax paper. Use the dish towel to help roll up the cake, folding the paper inside. Leave until really cool.

4 To use, gently unroll and spread with filling (don't add too much). Gently re-roll the cake, using paper or a dish towel as support. Place join-side underneath – on a board or serving plate and decorate as required.

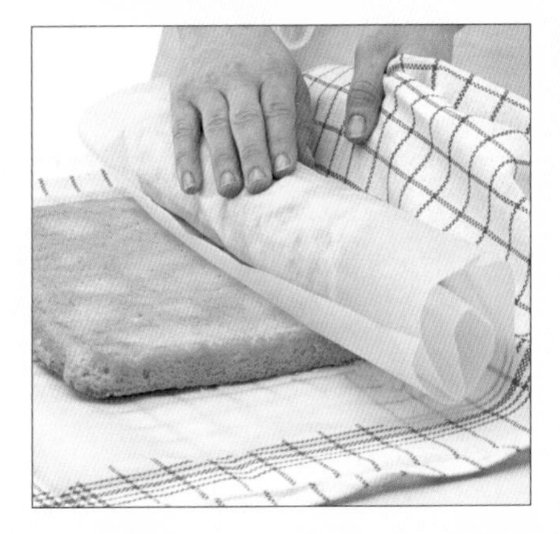

## A Simple Decoration for Sponge Cake

Sifting confectioners' sugar over a template makes a very quick, simple and stunning decoration. The easiest option is to sift the sugar over a paper doily, preferably one with a wide and open design. Alternatively, you can make a template by drawing a pattern on clean card or wax paper and cutting it out neatly. Be generous with the sugar to give a strong design or color the sugar with edible powder colors.

There's no need to reserve this star design for Christmas as it is ideal at any time. Find the template on page 96 and use only the center part for smaller cakes.

1 Dredge the top of the cake with confectioners' sugar. Place the central star and outer circle templates in position, laying them gently over the sugar. Dredge with unsweetened cocoa.

2 Use tweezers and a palette knife to remove the central star, taking care not to spill cocoa on the sugar.

3 Remove the outer circle template and transfer the cake to a plate.

# Madeira Cake

**The British Madeira cake evolved from the American pound cake, originally made with a pound in weight of each ingredient. It has become popular (known by various names) all around the world. It is a longer-keeping, firmer cake than a whisked or Victoria sponge cake. It is ideal for those who do not like rich fruit wedding cake, is perfect for making gâteau with several layers, and it freezes very well. Often baked in a loaf pan, it is a delicious, simple teatime cake, especially if you add a warm sugar and lemon crusted topping.**

**Makes one 7in round, 6in square or 2lb loaf cake**

1 cup butter or margarine, softened
1 cup superfine sugar
3 large eggs
2 cups all-purpose flour, sifted
1½ tsp baking powder
salt
1½ tsp vanilla extract (optional)

**Madeira Tip**

- To test if a Madeira or any deep Victoria sponge cake or light or rich fruit cake is cooked, push a metal skewer into the middle. If it comes out free of sticky mixture, the cake is ready.

**Variations**

***quantities for a 7in round or 6in square cake***

- **Lemon or orange:** Add the grated zest of 1 orange or lemon, or 1tbsp orange flower water.
- **Nuts:** Replace a quarter of the flour with finely ground nuts of your choice.
- **Seeds:** Add 2tbsp poppy, caraway or mixed seeds.
- **Cornmeal or Polenta:** Replace up to half the flour with ready-to-use cornmeal or polenta.

1 Grease and line a 7in round cake pan, or 6in square pan, or 2lb loaf pan. Preheat the oven to 180°C/350°F/gas mark 4. Beat the butter or margarine and sugar together until light and creamy. Gradually beat in the eggs until evenly blended.

2 Mix the sifted flour, baking powder and salt, and fold in gently using a large metal spoon. Add vanilla if required. Spoon the mixture into the prepared pan, level the top and bake for 1¼ hours, until a skewer pushed into the middle of the cake comes out clean and free of sticky mixture.

3 Remove the cake from the oven and leave to partly cool in the pan for 15–20 minutes. Then turn out onto a wire rack and leave to cool completely.

**Slicing a Madeira or Sponge Cake**

To slice a Madeira or sponge cake into several layers, allow it to cool completely. Chill a sponge cake briefly or Madeira for several hours if you need a fine, crumb-free cut. Place on a flat base – on a turntable if you have one – and place a sheet of wax paper on top so you do not leave finger indents. Use a large, sharp knife. Cut partly through, then give the cake a quarter-turn, keeping the knife in place, and continue cutting. Turn again and continue cutting until the cake is sliced through. The knife remains in the same position to produce even layers.

## Lemon Sugar Topping

Use this variation to make a simple weekend cake that may well be eaten before it has time to cool! Spooning the topping over takes seconds and it does not need a rich filling. Bake the cake in a loaf pan so it is easy to slice.

4tbsp lemon juice
1tbsp corn syrup
2tbsp granulated or crystal sugar

While the cake is still warm and in the pan, pierce it with a skewer, several times right the way through. Warm the lemon juice and syrup together. Add the sugar and immediately spoon the mixture over the cake, so the flavored syrup soaks through leaving some of the sugar crystals on the top.

**Madeira Tip**

- Madeira cake freezes well so make double quantities. Bake one quantity in a rectangular or square pan, and freeze it in slabs or sections. Use it for Iced Fancies (page 56) or for quick family desserts.
- Plain cake trimmings are great crumbled into a fruit crumble dessert topping.

**Madeira Proportions for Pan Sizes**

| *Pan* | *Fat* | *Superfine Sugar* | *Eggs* | *Baking Powder* | *All-purpose Flour* |
|---|---|---|---|---|---|
| 7in round or 6in square | 1 cup | 1 cup | 3 | 1½ tsp | 2 cups |
| 8in round or 7in square | 1¼ cups | 1¼ cups | 4 | 2tsp | 3 cups |
| 9in round or 8in square | 1¾ cups | 1¾ cups | 6 | 2½tsp | 4 cups |
| 10in round or 9in square | 2 cups | 2 cups | 7 | 3tsp | 4¾ cups |
| 12in round or 11in square | 2⅓ cups | 2⅓ cups | 10 | 4tsp | 6 cups |

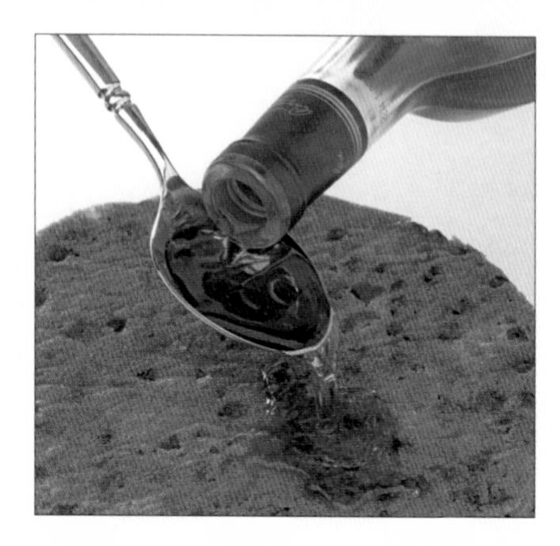

# Fruit Cakes

**A good homemade fruit cake is a rare treat these days, and festive occasions are incomplete without one. Why not make a small or individual fruit cake for a thank you or birthday gift for a special friend? It is better than any gift you might buy!**

## Dark Rich Fruit Cake

This dark and rich cake is made with dark ingredients – brown sugar, molasses, dark fruits – and traditionalists used to add gravy browning to ensure it was really dark! It is usually 'fed' with brandy before icing and can be kept for months, even years, thoroughly wrapped and stored in a cool dry place.

**Makes one 8in square cake or 9in round cake**

2lb mixed dried fruit
3/4 cup chopped mixed peel
1/2 cup candied cherries, chopped
1/2 cup pitted prunes, chopped
2-3tbsp sherry, brandy or rum
grated zest of 1 orange
grated zest of 1 lemon
3 cups all-purpose flour, sifted
1tsp ground cinnamon
1tsp ground mixed spice
1tsp salt
5 eggs
1 3/4 cups butter or margarine, softened
1 3/4 cups soft dark brown sugar
1tbsp molasses or corn syrup
Extra brandy to moisten the cooked cake

1 Prepare an 8in square or 9in round pan (page 11). Preheat the oven to 160°C/325°F/gas mark 3. In a large bowl, mix the dried fruit, peel, cherries, and prunes with the sherry, and orange and lemon zest. Leave to soak for 1–2 hours if possible to let the fruit soften and absorb the sherry.

2 Sift the flour, cinnamon, spice, and salt together. Lightly beat the eggs.

3 Cream the butter or margarine, sugar, and molasses together until paler and creamy. Gradually beat in the eggs, alternately adding the sifted flour in batches until it is well mixed.

4 Stir in the soaked fruits with any liquid from the bowl until evenly mixed. Spoon into the prepared pan and bake for 1 1/2 hours in the center of the oven.

5 Reduce the heat to 150°C/300°F/gas mark 2 and cook for a further 2 hours. If the cake begins to darken too quickly after the first hour, reduce the heat earlier.

6 Push a metal skewer into the middle of the cake to check that it is cooked. Leave to cool in the pan.

7 When cold, turn the cake out carefully. Overwrap thoroughly in double wax paper. Then wrap in foil and store in a cool place.

8 Remove the wax paper and pierce the cake with a fine metal skewer all over. Spoon a little brandy over the cake, allowing it to soak into the pierced holes.

**Feeding a fruit cake with brandy**

- To feed your cake with brandy, rum or whisky during storage, unwrap and prick the top several times with a fine skewer. Spoon over 2-3tbsp spirit, leave to soak in well before re-wrapping and storing. Repeat 2-3 times at weekly intervals.

# Golden Fruit Cake

This light golden fruit cake can be decorated within weeks of baking. Using the lighter fruits, such as pineapple, apricot, ginger and golden raisins, and soaking them well with fruit juice and rum, makes a cake that is wonderfully rich and moist but in a lighter and fruitier way compared to a traditional dark fruit cake. It's a matter of taste really!

**Makes one 8in round or 7in square cake**

- 1 1/2 cups mixed candied cherries, pineapple, ready-to-eat dried apricots, candied peel and/or crystallised ginger
- 1 1/4 cups golden raisins
- 1 1/4 cups raisins
- finely grated zest and juice of 1 small orange
- finely grated zest of 1 small lemon
- 2-3tbsp sherry, brandy or rum
- 1 1/4 cups butter or margarine, softened
- 1 1/4 cups superfine sugar
- 4 eggs
- 2 3/4 cups all-purpose flour, sifted
- 2tsp ground mixed spice
- 1 1/2 tsp baking powder

1 In a large bowl mix together all the fruit, zest, juice, and sherry, brandy or rum. Cover and set aside in a cold place for several hours or overnight.

2 Prepare an 8in round or 7in square pan (page 11). Preheat the oven to 160°C/325°F/gas mark 3. Cream the butter or margarine and sugar together in a large bowl until light and fluffy.

3 Beat the eggs together, then gradually stir them into the creamed mixture, adding the flour, mixed spice, and baking powder in batches alternately with egg.

4 Gently stir in the soaked fruit and any juices to make a fairly soft mixture. Spoon into the prepared pan.

5 Smooth the top of the mixture and bake for 1 1/2 hours, then reduce the heat to 150°C/300°F/gas mark 2 and bake for a further 1 hour. Check that the cake is cooked through. Cool in the pan.

6 Remove from the pan when cold and wrap in double-thick wax paper, then foil. Store in an airtight container until ready to decorate.

**To Test if Fruit Cake is Cooked**

- The cake should look slightly shrunk away from the sides of the pan. Press the top to check if it is firm.
- Push a clean metal skewer into the center of the cake, if it comes out with sticky mixture on it, return the cake to the oven.
- A fruit cake that is not fully cooked will definitely make a noise – a slight humming.

**Fruit and nut topping**

For a quick fruit cake decoration, simply arrange glacé fruits and whole nuts neatly on top of the matured cake and brush with corn syrup or honey.

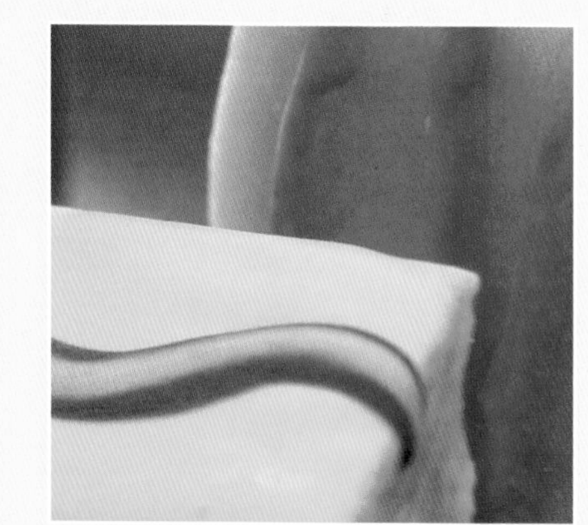

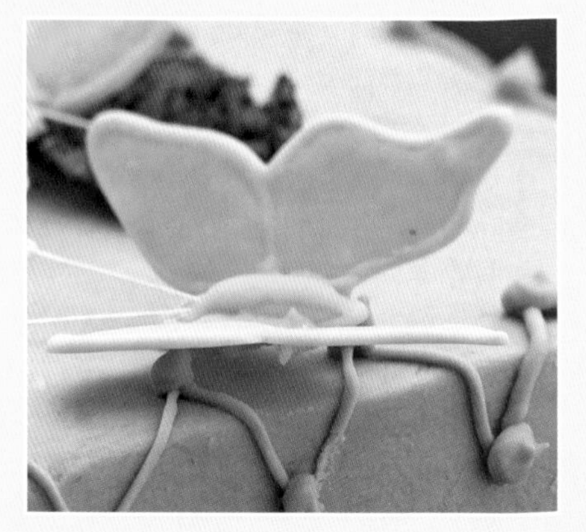

# Decorating with Style

The fun part of making a cake is the decorating and finishing. Seeing your idea or design come to fruition, and hearing the appreciation of family and friends, is what it's all about. Whether you have spent a couple of hours or a couple of days creating the cake, the end result is what matters.

Map the design fully before you start so that you can assemble colors, tools, trimmings and any specialist items. If you haven't used a technique before, take time to try it out before working on the cake. Allow for breakages by making extra decorations. Plan your work in stages, working backward from the day the cake is required to the baking day.

Drying time is among the most important stages – for marzipan to harden, frosting to set, and sugar paste to firm up. Any delicate decorations, flowers and cut-outs will need at least 1-2 days to dry before they can be assembled on the final cake. Do not forget to plan for setting and drying or you may run out of time.

# Decorating with Royal Icing

**Royal icing was created for royal occasions, and often used for very intricate designs far too complex and time consuming for the majority of today's requirements. However, a traditional occasion, for example a wedding, calls for something really special by way of a decorated cake, and many people like the royal icing finish. Royal icing more versatile than it first appears to be. It can be used for delicate, simple designs that are modern and do not require great skill or too much practice. Getting the consistency right for piping royal icing is vital, particularly if you are decorating several cakes or tiers – as your wrists will ache if the icing is too stiff.**

**Royal Icing Tips**

- Be well organised and have everything you will need at hand before you start working with royal icing.
- Make up sufficient icing in the first place, to be able to use it to firm up a small quantity of thinned icing that has become too soft.
- Remember not to add glycerine or liquid glucose for piping or run-outs – the decorations must set hard.
- Keep all bowls or bags of colored mixture covered with plastic wrap or a damp cloth at all times.
- Use a damp, fine paintbrush to correct (rub out or gently brush off) any minor piping errors, or pull out the points or corners of flowers.
- Mix the required color, then check the consistency and add a little of the original batch of royal icing to firm up the icing, or single drops of water to loosen or thin the icing slightly.

## Soft Peak

This is the basic consistency for flat icing a marzipan-covered cake. The icing should hold a peak that just falls over slightly at the tip.

## Full or Firm Peak

Suitable for most piping tasks. The icing peaks stay firm and sharp. Don't make it too firm or it will be difficult to pipe.

## Very Firm Peak

This is the ideal consistency for a Christmas snow scene. Keep working in more confectioners' sugar until it stands up in stiff, short sharp peaks.

## Run-out Icing

For outlining a template the icing needs to be almost as stiff as soft peak – maybe a touch softer.

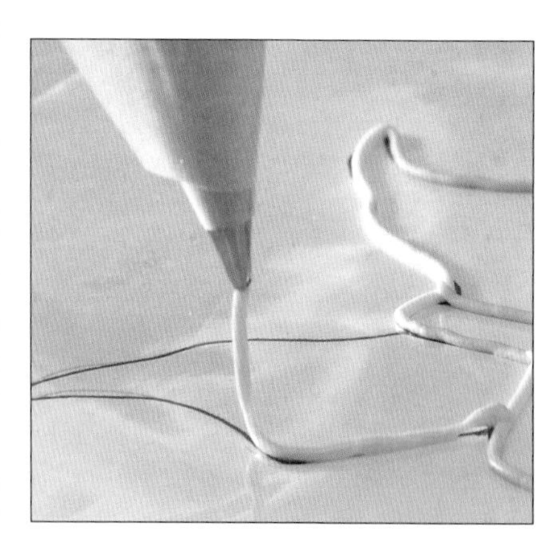

## Flooding Consistency

To 'flood' a shape, the icing needs to be much looser. To test, spoon a little into a bowl and the lines and edges of any peaks should fade within 8 seconds.

# To Make and Fill a Piping Bag

You can never have too many small piping bags. Even though you may buy ready made bags, there will be occasions when you need to make one.

1 Start with a square of waxed paper, approximately 10in square. Fold in half into two triangles. Crease from the middle of the long side to the point.

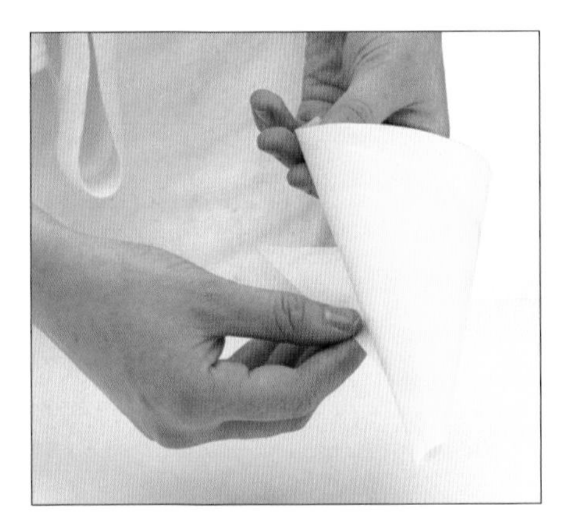

2 Holding the points opposite the long side with one hand, roll the left corner over to line up with them. Do the same with the other corner so it wraps around, making a cone with all the points neatly together.

3 Shuffle the points until they meet neatly. Ensure the cone has a good shape, with a firm point at the bottom.

4 Fold over and secure the points you are holding with tape or a staple clip. If you are using a nozzle, snip a little off the tip of the bag and insert the nozzle.

5 Only half fill with icing. Then fold over the top to enclose the icing.

6 Fold the corners firmly in toward the middle, and fold the top over again. Gently squeeze the icing down into the nozzle. If you are not using a nozzle, cut off a tiny point from the tip of the piping bag equivalent to the size of the nozzle you need.

**Nozzles**

- For fine lines use a small plain nozzle, no. 1 or 2.
- For small rosettes, stars or shells use a no. 5, 7, 9, or 11.
- For ropes use a 42, 43, or 44.

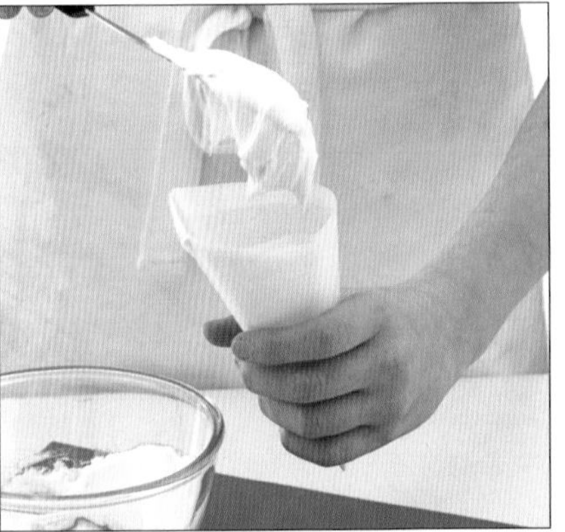

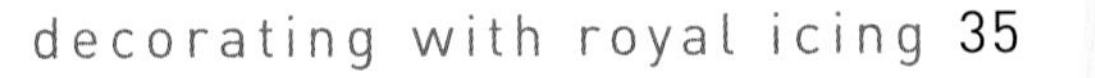

# Iced Cup Cakes

**The great thing about making lots of little cakes is you can vary the toppings to suit your guests, your children, or your mood, and have fun with several different ideas at the same time.**

**Makes about 15**

1 x 3-egg quantity Victoria Sponge Cake mixture (page 16)
1-2tsp unsweetened cocoa powder
2-3tsp milk
5 cherries with stalks
2 quantities Glacé Icing (page 24)
2tbsp Chocolate Buttercream (page 23)
5 chocolate shapes (page 43)
confectioners' sugar, sifted
red or blue edible food coloring
silver dragees
coloured stars

1 Preheat the oven to 180°C/350°F/gas mark 4. Prepare the sponge cake mixture. Prepare 15 paper cup cake cases in a muffin pan. Mix the unsweetened cocoa powder with the milk and use to flavor about one third of the mixture. Spoon the mixtures into the cake cases and bake for 15-20 minutes until evenly risen, lightly browned, and just firm to the touch. Transfer to a wire rack and leave until cold.

2 Set aside five plain cakes, selecting those that are more domed. Color 1tbsp of the glacé icing red or blue. Spoon white glacé icing over the remaining plain cup cakes. Add drops of colored icing and then swirl the colored icing into the white with a toothpick. Finish with silver dragees or colored stars.

3 Place a cherry on each of the reserved plain cakes, keeping them in place with a little glacé icing. Holding the cherry stalk to keep the fruit in place, pour about 1tbsp glacé icing over the cherry. Add extra icing if necessary, to coat the cake. Leave to set firm.

4 Cut a small lid off the top of each chocolate cake. Pipe a swirl of buttercream into the center of each. Replace the lid on top. Add a chocolate shape and sift a little confectioners' sugar over the top.

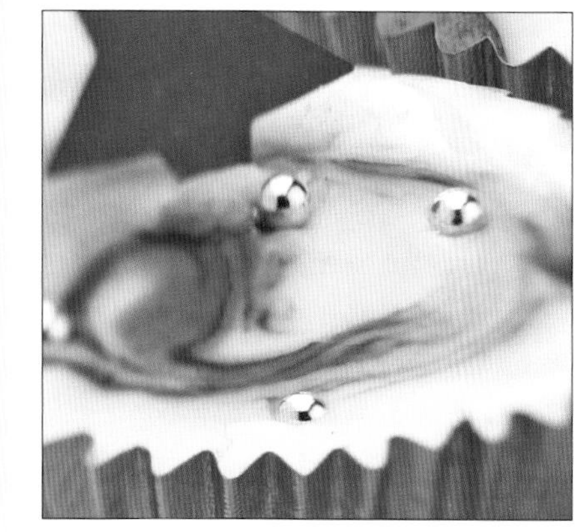

# Frosted Fruits Gâteau

**Most fruits take sugar frosting but the smaller fruit on stalks look the best. Autumn berries are good if they are still firm. Any very soft or slightly blemished fruit will not work well as they do not dry out fully. When well coated with sugar fruit will keep for several days in a dry atmosphere.**

**Serves 6-8**

6oz mixed firm berries
4oz mixed fruits, such as cherries, redcurrants and physallis
1 small egg white
$^{1}/_{2}$ cup superfine sugar
7in Genoese Sponge Cake (page 17)
$1^{1}/_{2}$ cups heavy cream

1 Set aside the softer and larger berries for the filling, cutting them in half if necessary. Dry the fruit thoroughly on paper towel.

2 Put the egg white in a small bowl and beat very slightly to loosen it. Put the sugar in a larger bowl. Cover a clean tray with wax paper.

3 Brush the fruit thinly with egg white, brushing the egg white into the cracks and crevices.

4 Then coat thoroughly in the sugar by dipping the fruit and sprinkling with sugar. Place on the wax paper. Leave in a warm dry place for several hours or until the sugar coating is completely dry and crisp.

5 Whisk the cream until it stands in soft peaks. Sandwich the sponge cake layers with about a third of the cream, and the reserved berries. Spread a little cream over the top and pipe the rest around the top edge of the cake.

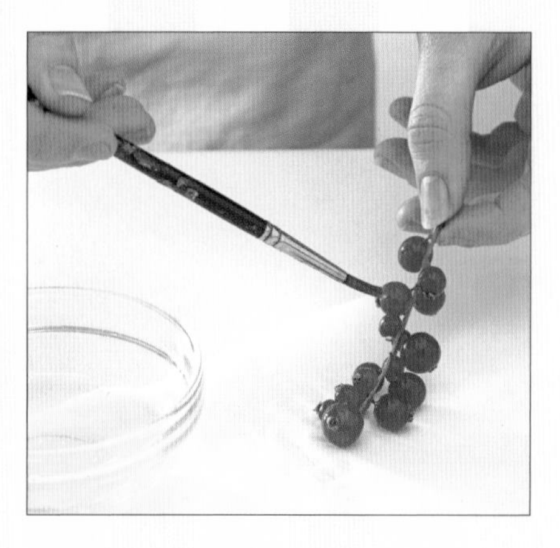

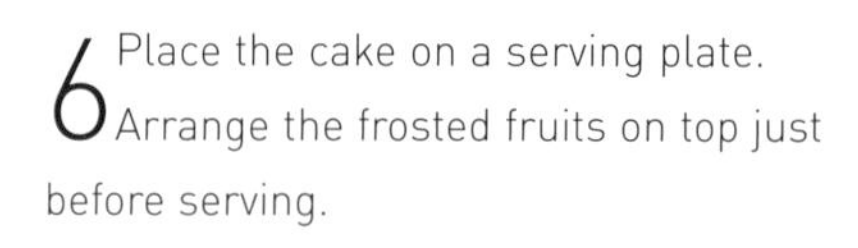

6 Place the cake on a serving plate. Arrange the frosted fruits on top just before serving.

**Sugar Coating Tips**

- Fruit should be clean and dry.
- Repeat the coating process for the best result.
- For longer keeping, store the fruit in an airtight container. Add a little salt or silica crystals wrapped in a twist of cheesecloth to absorb any moisture.

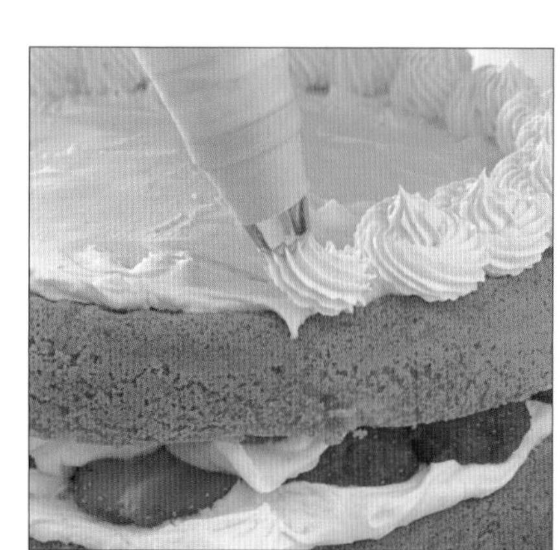

# Carrot Cake

**This moist cake is covered in a rich and naughty topping. The decorative marzipan carrots and cinnamon sticks are fun to make, especially as they can be prepared well ahead and stored in an airtight container.**

**Serves 16**

- 3/4 cup sunflower oil
- 3/4 cup soft light brown sugar
- 3 large eggs, beaten
- finely grated zest of 1 orange and juice of 1/2 orange
- 1 1/2 cups whole-wheat self-rising flour
- 1tsp baking powder
- 1 cup golden raisins
- 1 1/2 cups finely grated carrots

**Topping and decoration**

- 1 quantity American Frosting (page 25)
- 3 1/2oz Marzipan (page 26)
- brown and terracotta edible food colorings
- angelica or glacé lime peel

1 Make the decorations first. Color two-thirds of the marzipan terracotta and use to make carrots (see page 44). Use a toothpick to mark the characteristic indents and brush a little coloring into the cracks. Push tiny sticks of angelica or glacé lime peel into the tops for stalks.

2 Color the rest of the marzipan brown and roll out thinly. Roll tiny pieces into sticks to resemble cinnamon sticks, then cut or fray the edges. Leave to dry out.

3 Preheat the oven to 180°C/350°F/gas mark 4. Line and grease a 9in round pan. Blend all the cake ingredients in a bowl and beat thoroughly. Spoon the mixture into the prepared pan and smooth it evenly.

4 Bake for 40-50 minutes, until the cake is risen and firm to the touch. Leave to cool in the pan then transfer to a wire rack.

5 Prepare the American frosting. Spread the frosting all over the cake, peaking and swirling it attractively. Place on a serving dish. Arrange the carrots and cinnamon sticks on the cake shortly before serving.

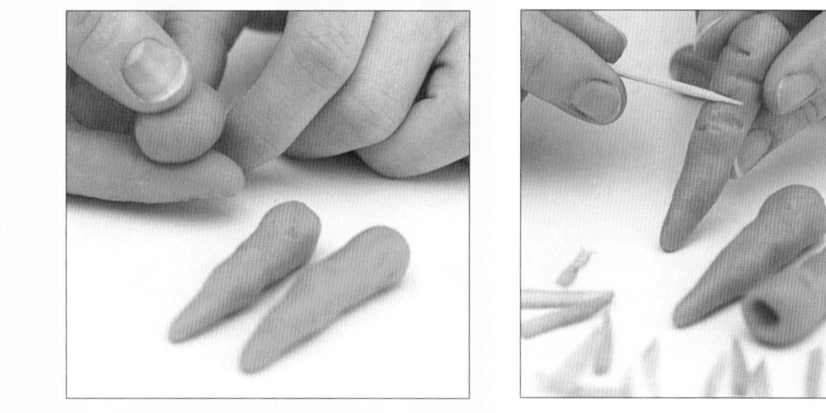

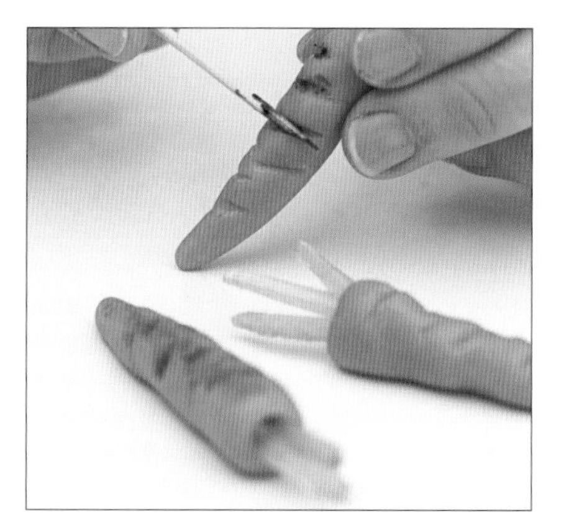

# Tipsy Chocolate Treat

**Serves 8-10**

9 squares bitter chocolate
3/4 cup dairy butter
6 eggs, separated
1 cup superfine sugar
1/2 cup self-rising flour
3-4tbsp rum

**Icing and Decoration**

1 quantity bitter chocolate Ganache (page 41)
3 squares white chocolate
4 squares bitter chocolate

**This indulgent, grown-up chocolate cake is well laced with rum underneath the drizzled chocolate decoration.**

1 Line and grease a deep 8in round loose-bottomed pan. Preheat the oven to 170°C/325°F/gas mark 3. Melt the chocolate and butter gently in a heatproof bowl over a saucepan of hot water. Alternatively, melt in the microwave for 30–50 seconds at a time on medium. Leave to cool slightly.

2 Whisk the egg yolks with 3/4 cup of the sugar until pale, thick and creamy. Gently stir in the cooled chocolate. Then fold in the flour.

3 In a separate bowl, whisk the egg whites until stiff but not dry. Then gently whisk in the rest of the sugar. Fold the whites into the chocolate mixture and spoon the mixture into the prepared pan.

4 Bake for 1 hour 15 minutes, until the cake is well risen and springy to the touch. A knife should come out clean and free of sticky mixture. Leave to part-cool in the pan, then turn out onto a wire rack and leave until cold.

5 Invert the cake and sprinkle the rum over its base. Allow to soak in for a few minutes. Then turn the cake the right way up on the rack. Stand the rack over a tray or paper. Reserve a third of the ganache. Quickly pour the rest all over the cake. Make sure all the cake is covered, and save the drips of excess ganache that have fallen onto the tray or paper.

7 Cut a piece of foil and mark a rectangle about 10in x 3in on it. Have a rolling pin ready. Melt the white and bitter chocolate separately and spoon into small paper piping bags. Snip off the points for piping finely. Drizzle white chocolate in lines across the top of the cake.

8 Drizzle the bitter chocolate on the foil first, then the white chocolate, keeping within the marked rectangle. Reserve the unused chocolate. Carefully drape the foil over the rolling pin and leave to set. When firm, carefully remove pieces of the drizzled chocolate semi-circles and arrange several on top of the cake.

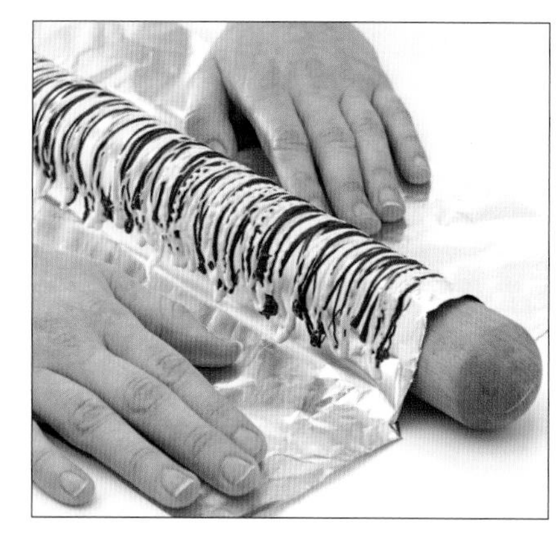

9 Transfer the cake to a serving plate. Re-melt the remaining ganache and chocolate together and allow to cool until thick enough to pipe. Then pipe around the base of the cake. Keep in a cool place until ready to serve.

# Retro Iced Fancies

**Originally called *fondant fancies,* and covered with a soft pouring fondant, these favorites of a bygone era seem to have taken on a new lease of life. Here they are coated with soft royal icing instead of the traditional fondant. Glacé icing will not do. They can be made in whatever shape and color you like, but look particularly attractive in soft pastel shades.**

**Makes 10-12**

2-egg Victoria Sponge Cake baked in a 6in square or a rectangular pan (page 16)
1/2 quantity Royal Icing (page 28)
edible food coloring
few blanched almonds or pieces of candied peel

1 Cut the cake into bite-size squares, circles, triangles, or other shapes, such as crescents, and diamonds. Place on a wire rack.

2 Divide the icing among three bowls. Keep one portion white and cover it closely with plastic wrap. Color the other two portions as you wish, then gently dilute them with a little water or lemon juice to a pouring consistency – just a little thicker than for run-outs.

3 Coat half the batch of cakes with one color and half with the other. If the coats are thin, repeat once the first coat has dried. Place a piece of peel or an almond on some of the cakes before you coat them.

4 Color the reserved white icing two or more different colors and use to pipe or drizzle designs on the cakes. Leave one color to set fully before adding another color. Leave to set before serving.

**Fondant Tip**

Fondant can be bought as a packet mix from specialty cake decorating suppliers. It can be made up as directed and used for these iced fancies for a truly authentic effect.

# Orange and Lemon Gâteau

**What can you do with a frozen sponge cake? Simple, slice the layers and sandwich them together with tangy lemon curd. Coat in a fruity buttercream and top with candied shreds of orange rind and shards of caramelized sugar. Nothing to it really!**

**Serves 10–12**

- 5 or 6 thin layers lemon Victoria Sponge Cake (page 16) or Madeira Cake (page 18)
- 2 quantities lemon Buttercream (page 23) or Meringue Buttercream (page 24)
- 1 large orange
- 1/2 cup superfine sugar
- 2tbsp orange juice
- 6tbsp lemon curd
- 1/4 cup granulated sugar
- 10in round gold cake board

1 Chill the thin cake layers. Prepare the buttercream and leave to firm up.

2 Use a vegetable peeler to cut thin strips of orange rind, avoiding the white pith or trimming it off. Then cut into fine strips. Dissolve the caster sugar in the orange juice in a small saucepan. Add the strips of rind and simmer gently until the sugar has almost caramelized, and all the liquid has evaporated.

3 Tip the rinds onto a sheet of non-stick baking paper. Separate the strands and leave in an airy room that is not too cool or damp, until hardened.

4 Sandwich the sponge cake layers together alternately with lemon curd and a third of the buttercream. Lightly cover the top and sides with buttercream, finishing with a simple swirled or knife-mark pattern. Chill until ready to serve.

5 Meanwhile, sprinkle the granulated sugar on a small sheet of foil. Place under a hot grill until the sugar has dissolved and is bubbling and golden brown. Set aside to cool.

6 Place the cake on the board. Just before serving arrange the shreds of orange rind in a pile in the center of the cake. Break the caramel into shards or large pieces. Arrange some caramel pieces with the orange rind on top and some around the edge of the cake.

# Battenberg Cake

**This unique cake is ideal for lovers of marzipan. It was apparently named after the marriage of Queen Victoria's granddaughter to Prince Louis of Battenberg in 1884. Our recipe has a choice of three flavor combinations.**

**Serves 6-8**

1 x 4-egg Victoria Sponge Cake mixture (page 16) flavored and colored with vanilla; orange and chocolate; or lemon and orange
2-3tbsp apricot jelly
10oz Marzipan (page 26), flavored with 3tbsp sifted unsweetened cocoa powder for the chocolate cake
pink and green edible food coloring if making the vanilla cake

1 Preheat the oven to 180°C/350°F/gas mark 4. Line and grease a 7in shallow square baking pan. Cut a strip of double wax paper and grease it. Use this to divide the pan in half.

2 Prepare the sponge cake mixture, flavor it with vanilla, if liked, and divide in half. Color the vanilla portions pink and green. Alternatively, instead of vanilla, use chocolate in one portion and orange in the other; or lemon in one portion and orange in the other. Color the orange portion with a little orange food coloring.

3 Spoon one mixture into half the prepared baking pan, keeping the paper in the middle, and the rest in the other side. Try to make the divide as straight as possible. Bake in the middle of the oven for 35-40 minutes. Turn out and cool on a wire rack.

4 When cool, trim the edges and cut the cake portions lengthwise in half, making four equal parts. Warm the jelly in a small saucepan. Brush two sides of each portion of cake with jelly and stick them together to give a effect.

5 Roll out the marzipan to a rectangle wide and long enough to wrap around the cake. Trim the edges neatly. Brush the outside of the cake with jelly. Place the cake on the marzipan and wrap the paste around the cake. Dampen the edges lightly to form a neat join at one of the corners of the cake.

6 Pinch the top and bottom edges of the paste into a pattern with crimpers. Use the extra marzipan to make marzipan flowers and leaves in various colors or other decorations of your choice.

# Sunburst

**Something to celebrate – a christening or a new house perhaps? Whatever the reason, bring some added sunshine to the occasion with this quick and simple, three-dimensional design with sparkle and silver shimmer.**

**Serves: 16-20**

8in square Golden Fruit Cake (page 21)
2tbsp Apricot Glaze (page 26)
8oz Marzipan (optional, page 26)
1½lb Sugar Paste (page 30)
yellow and blue edible food colors
blue sequin ribbon
yellow sparkles
silver moon dust
turquoise balls
10in square cake board

1 Brush the cake with apricot glaze, then cover with the marzipan, if using, or cover with sugar paste alone. Use about two-thirds of the sugar paste to cover the cake, reserving the rest for decoration. Transfer the cake to the board.

2 Color two-thirds of the remaining sugar paste pale turquoise (using blue and yellow) and one-third pale yellow. Wrap in plastic wrap. Roll out a quarter of the turquoise paste and use to cover the board. Then frill the edge with a toothpick or frilling tool (page 40). Trim the base of the cake and the board with sequin ribbon.

3 Roll out the yellow paste quite thickly and cut a 1½-2in circle for the sun. Cut out 7-8 strips shaped from narrow to wide for the sun's rays. Attach the sun and the rays to the top of the cake with a little water.

4 Roll out the rest of the turquoise paste quite thickly and cut out a variety of cloud-like shapes. Use the blunt ends of different-sized round cutters and the wide ends of piping nozzles to make the shapes and cut a third of the circle. Use a fine, sharp, pointed knife to cut out the marked shapes of larger clouds. Cut away some of the centers to increase the curve. Layer the clouds over the sun's rays, raising some pieces for a three dimensional effect. Cut several tiny raindrops from the remaining blue paste.

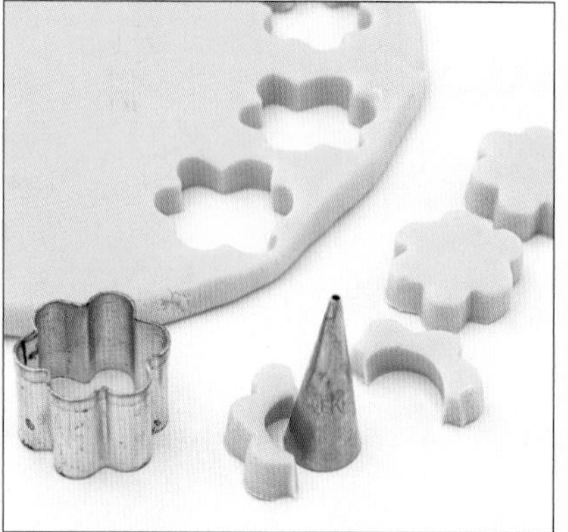

5 Sprinkle the sun with yellow sparkles. Using a damp brush, brush the clouds with moon dust. Finally, place the turquoise balls on the board at the base of the cake with a little icing.

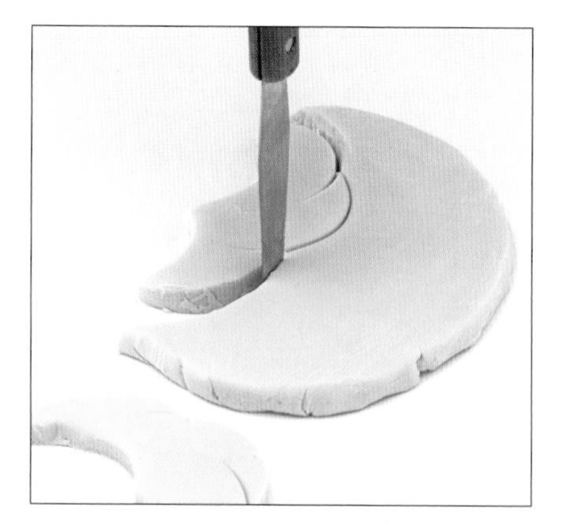

# Chocolate Heaven

**A glamorous casing of chocolate ganache and a topping of tiny alcoholic truffles transform a simple chocolate sponge cake into a stunning dinner party gâteau or centerpiece for almost any occasion.**

**Serves 8-12**

- $1^1/_4$ cups heavy cream
- 2-4tbsp brandy, whisky or Courvoisier
- 7in chocolate Genoese Sponge Cake (page 17)
- 1 quantity Ganache (page 41)
- $^1/_4$ cup confectioners' sugar, sifted
- $^1/_4$ cup unsweetened cocoa powder, sifted
- Chocolate Leaves (page 42)

1 Whip the cream lightly. Take a third of the cream and stir in half the brandy, whisky, or Courvoisier. Sandwich the sponge cake layers together with this and place on a serving plate.

2 Cut a strip of foil at least the length of the cake circumference, and twice the height of the side. Spread one third of the warm ganache over this, making the base edge straight along the foil, but the top edge attractively jagged. Leave to set but do not allow to become hard.

3 Divide the remaining ganache in half. Beat half the remaining cream into one portion of ganache and continue to beat lightly until it thickens to a spreading consistency. Swirl this over the top of the cake and spread it around the sides.

4 For the truffles, mix the remaining ganache with the remaining alcohol and cream, and the confectioners' sugar. Beat well, then place in the refrigerator to set.

5 Wrap the just-set chocolate case around the cake, jagged edge up, and gently peel off the foil as you press the chocolate onto the cake. Press the edges to seal. Chill the cake until the chocolate is firm.

6 Dust your hands with cocoa and roll small teaspoons of the truffle mixture into tiny balls. Chill again. When ready to serve, carefully arrange the truffles on the top of the cake, adding some on the serving plate. Dust with more cocoa powder and finish with a few chocolate leaves.

# Berrytime

**Realistic-looking three-dimensional raspberries, bramble berries and tayberries can all be made by hand with a little time and patience. Individual berries can be wired together with leaves. Flat, or bas relief, berries, to fit on the vertical sides of a cake, can be made in flexible plastic molds. Molds are also available for making detailed clusters of berries and leaves. A combination of molds and cutters works well.**

**Serves 10-12**

8in round Golden Fruit Cake (page 21)
1lb Marzipan (page 26)
1½lb Sugar Paste (page 30)
Raspberry pink, blackberry and leaf green gel or dust colors
8oz bought flower paste mix
floristry wire (24-26 gauge)
green and brown floristry tape (known as gutta percha)
edible glue
10in square cake board

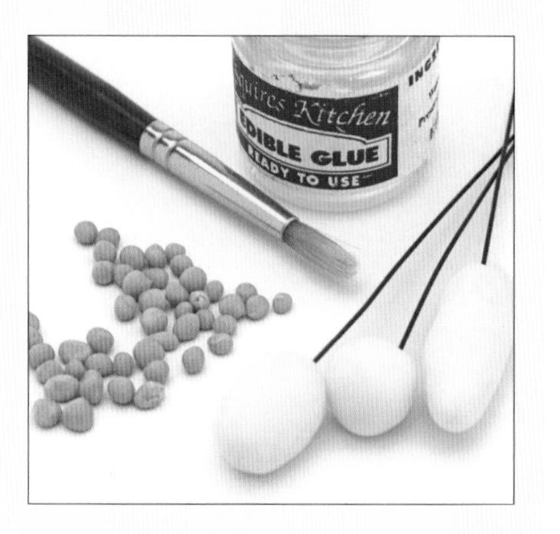


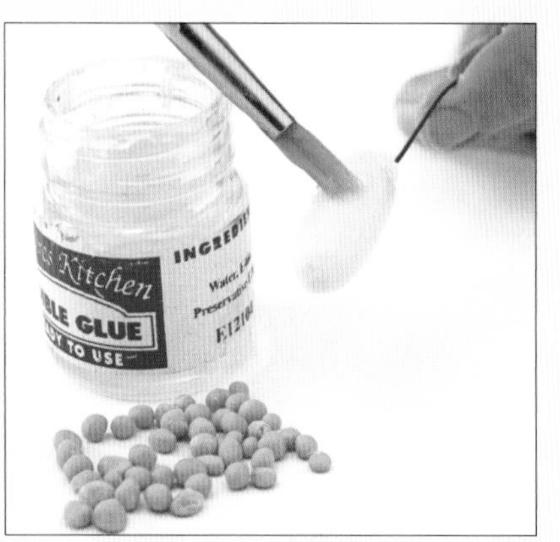


1 Cover the cake with marzipan. Color three quarters of the sugar paste a shade of raspberry pink and use to cover the cake. Cover the board with white sugar paste and top with sugar paste that you have colored grass green.

2 Make up the flower paste according to the packet instructions. Knead until thoroughly workable. Use about a quarter to fill individual berry molds lightly dusted with cornstarch, if using. Turn out and leave to harden in a warm dry place for at least 24 hours. Paint the shapes the colors of the berries and leaves using diluted gel or dry powders.

3 Color about a quarter of the remaining flower paste a shade of raspberry pink. Mold about 15 pea-sized round or pear-shaped white balls for cores and attach them to 6in lengths floristry wire. To do this, make a tiny hook at one end of the wire to hold paste and moisten the wire with glue. Leave to dry for 1-2 hours.

4 For each berry roll 20-30 tiny balls of pink paste and attach them to the cores with glue. Shape gently with your fingers and leave to dry for 1-2 hours. Support the wires in a block of floristry foam while the paste is drying.

5 For the calyx (the leafy cup which holds the berry), color the rest of the paste leaf green. Roll out a small piece of paste thinly and cut out a small calyx. Gently flatten out the points with a dog-bone tool. Place the paste on a piece of foam and then push in the center to give it a cup shape. Push a berry wire through the center, brush the paste with glue, and secure the calyx to the berry. Bend the points with a paintbrush to give a life-like shape.

6 Cut out several leaves from the green sugar paste. Vein them with a vein marker and shape them gently, then attach to wires with glue. Leave everything to set hard under a lamp for 24 hours.

7 Tint the berries and leaves with shades of purple and green-brown, respectively. Take 2-3 berries and 2-3 leaves, and wrap their wires together with green tape to make a small bunch.

8 Arrange the bunches and the molded fruits on and around the cake, attaching them with edible glue.

# Petal Power Cake

**This charming flower-covered creation is perfect for Mother's day instead of a bunch of flowers. Use freesias instead of roses, if you like, and color the cake to match the colors of the petals.**

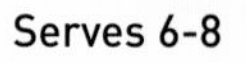

**Serves 6-8**

8in Madeira Cake or Golden Fruit Cake (pages 18 or 21)
2tbsp Apricot Glaze (page 26)
12oz Marzipan (page 26)
1lb Sugar Paste (page 30)
3-4 roses in full bloom
1 small egg white, lightly beaten
2tbsp superfine sugar
edible food colors to match roses
edible leaf green dusting powder
10in round cake board

1 Using the template on page 96, cut the cake into a petal shape. Brush with apricot glaze and cover with marzipan. Set aside for several hours. Cover the board with colored paper to match the flowers if you wish.

2 Discard any blemished petals and put the best ones on a board covered with wax paper. Save the buds or centers of the roses to decorate the board.

3 Brush the petals thinly with egg white. Then sprinkle them with sugar to coat them evenly and fairly thickly. Leave on the paper for several hours to dry and harden.

4 Color the remaining sugar paste to match the petals, marbling the colors if you wish. Remove about a fifth of the paste, then cover the cake with the rest. Place the cake on the board.

5 Using a sugar paste gun and the reserved colored or white sugar paste, make sufficient rope to wrap around the edge of the cake. The white paste can be colored first, if liked. Twist two lengths of different-colored ropes together for an attractive effect.

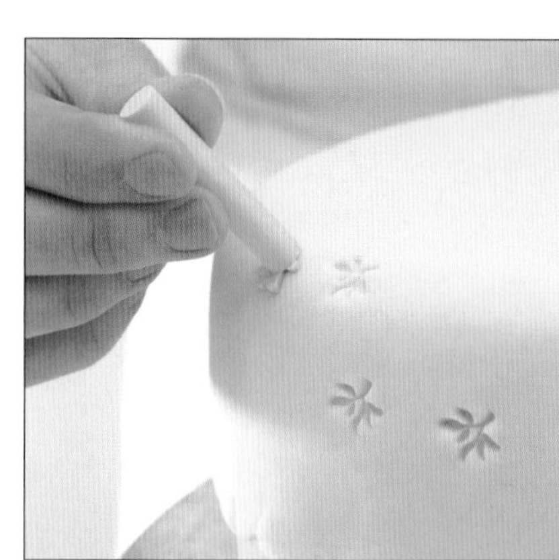

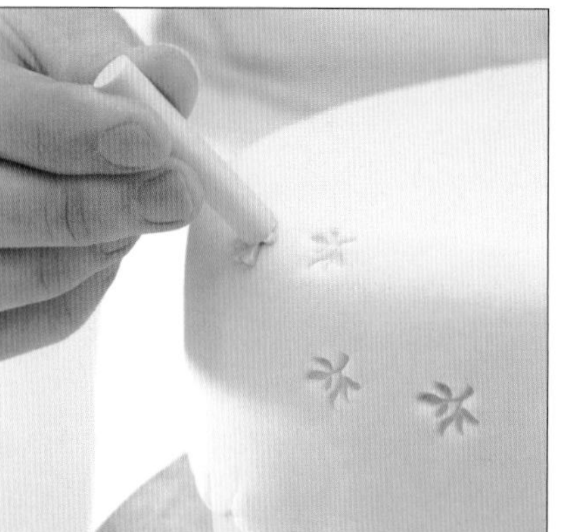

6 Use a tiny flower embosser to mark a delicate pattern all over the cake. Brush a little dusting powder in a pale leaf green into these indents (page 40).

7 Arrange a selection of sugared petals on top of the cake and on the board. Add the reserved flower buds for a finishing touch.

**Storing sugared roses**

Sugared rose petals will keep well in an airtight container for a couple of weeks. To help keep them dry, add a little salt or silica crystals tied up in a small piece of cheesecloth to absorb moisture.

# Butterfly Thank You Cake

**Individual cakes make the perfect gift, particularly as a Thank You. Why not make one large square cake and cut it into four? Freeze the remaining sections so you always have a small cake ready to be transformed into an impromptu gift.**

**Serves 2-4**

4in square Dark Rich Fruit Cake or Madeira Cake (pages 20 or 18)
1tbsp Apricot Glaze (page 26)
6oz Marzipan (page 26)
1/2 quantity Royal Icing (page 28) plus 1 quantity Royal Icing without glycerine
pink and hyacinth edible food color powders
white stamens and colored stamens
2-3 prepared leaves

1 Brush the cake with apricot glaze and cover with marzipan. Leave to dry for 24 hours. Over the next couple of days give the cake one coat of white and two coats of lavender royal icing. Leave to dry thoroughly.

2 Meanwhile, make up the royal icing without glycerine. Color half pink and half a light lavender color. Use pink and hyacinth colors to achieve the right shades. Using the template on page 96 and run-out instructions on page 37, make 6-8 of the small flat run-out butterflies in lavender with pink dots. Leave to in a cool place to harden.

3 Make 3-4 medium-sized pink butterfly run-out pieces with lavender dots. Attach white stamens to the body while still wet. Leave to dry. Pipe a tiny amount of pink icing on either side of the body pieces and attach the wings. Raise the wings slightly and support them on a soft curved surface so they dry raised.

4 Use some of the remaining lavender icing to pipe tiny dots and lines around the top edge of the cake. Attach a small bunch of colored stamens and two leaves to the top of the cake. Position one butterfly on the bunch of stamens. Add as many more butterflies as you wish, attaching smaller ones around the sides. Butterflies can be attached to a gift box for the cake.

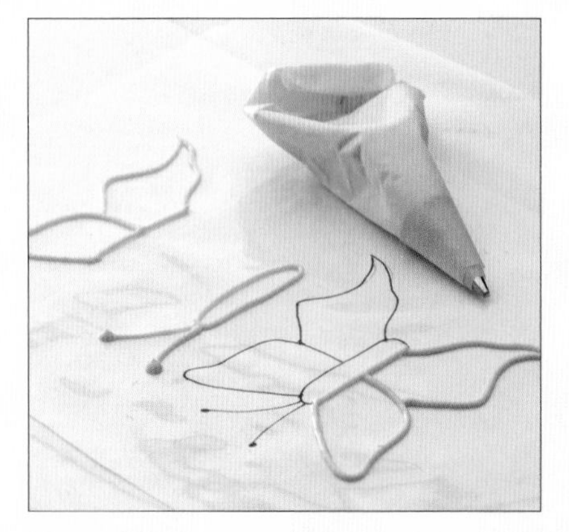

5 Support the cake on folds of matching tissue paper and place in a small cake box.

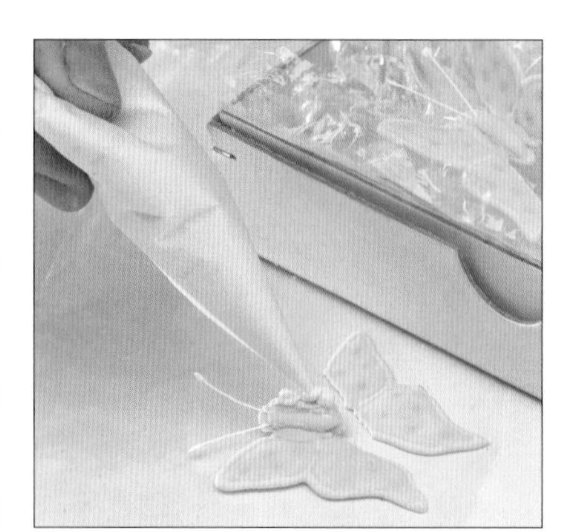

# 21st Birthday

**Everyone loves a cup cake and this impressive collection suits any age, and almost any occasion. A good strong color theme is important; matched with lots of ideas for the individual toppings and you have a fun recipe for success. Make plenty of cakes, as they are sure to go!**

**Makes about 30**

1 quantity Carrot Cake mixture (page 52)
silver cup cake cases
1lb Royal Icing (page 28)
blue edible food coloring
2oz Sugar Paste (page 30)
silver candles, balls, ribbons and/or netting to decorate
edible blue or sliver glitter
blue and silver ribbon
two- or three-tier cake stand

1 Preheat the oven to 180°C/350°F/gas mark 4. Place 30 silver cake cases in small muffin pans. Make the carrot cake mixture and divide it among the cake cases. Bake for about 20 minutes, until evenly risen, lightly browned and springy to touch. Allow to cool on wire racks.

2 Color half the royal icing pale blue. Coat half the cakes with white icing and half with blue. Top some of the cakes with silver balls, arranged in '21' shapes, while the icing is wet. Leave to set for several hours or overnight.

3 Color or marble the sugar paste with blue. Roll out half thinly and cut out star or flower shapes. Roll the rest of the paste into ropes and shape into the numerals one and two, small enough to fit on the cakes. Leave these decorations to dry.

4 Color some of the royal icing a darker shade of blue. Choose a variety of piped designs, such as dots, lattice, diagonal lines, circles and flowers, and decorate five or more cakes in similar designs, using different colorways. Simple designs using contrasting colors are very effective. Add numbers, stars, candles, streamers and/or glitter, to some of the cakes. Use a limited number of different designs and make several cakes of each type. Leave to set.

5 To serve, arrange all the cakes in a pile on a two- or three-tiered cake stand. Make sure cakes with candles are stable and upright. Tie a big ribbon around the base of the stand and light the candles.

**Cup cake tip**

Bite-size cup cakes are stylish and fun. Make them in petit four cases, reducing the cooking time to 10-15 minutes. Keep all the decorations miniature in proportion with the tiny cakes.

21
21
21
21
21

# Valentine's Cake

**Fine candy-colored stripes are easy and effective. A few silver balls and a centerpiece of sugar paste hearts finish this stylish design for a striking result.**

**Serves 6-8**

1 quantity Madeira Cake (page 18) baked in a 7-8in heart-shaped pan
3tbsp Apricot Glaze (page 26) or Buttercream (page 23)
12oz Marzipan (page 26)
1lb Sugar Paste (page 30)
edible glue
silver balls
pink ribbon
11in heart-shaped cake board

1 Brush the cake with apricot glaze and cover with marzipan. Leave to dry for 12-24 hours. Color two-thirds of the sugar paste a very pale pink and cover the cake with this. Keep any leftover sugar paste in a small polythene bag.

2 Measure the cake diagonally across the middle and down both sides. Color the rest of the sugar paste candy pink and roll it out to a thick strip about 3in wide and the length measured. Cut into several thin strips.

3 Starting at the middle of the cake, which will require the longest strip, use a ruler to paint a straight line of glue across the top of the cake and down the sides. Place the strip of paste in position. Press gently into place. Lay the remaining strips across the cake in the same way. Keep the strips 1in apart. Measure the positions precisely for straight, even lines. Cut the strips off neatly at the base. Save any excess sugar paste.

4 Place the cake on a heart-shaped board covered with white tissue paper or white sugar paste. Roll out the remaining sugar paste thickly and cut-out heart shapes in various sizes. Attach tiny hearts around the base of the board and slightly larger hearts on the cake.

5 Cut out a few large hearts. Cut out some hollow middles by using a smaller heart-shaped cutter. Attach small heart shapes to some of the larger shapes. Leave the shapes to harden – they are to stand up in the center of the cake. The large hearts should be supported on soft icing or attached to the cake with glue. Finally, add silver balls around the base of the cake and trim the board with pink ribbon.

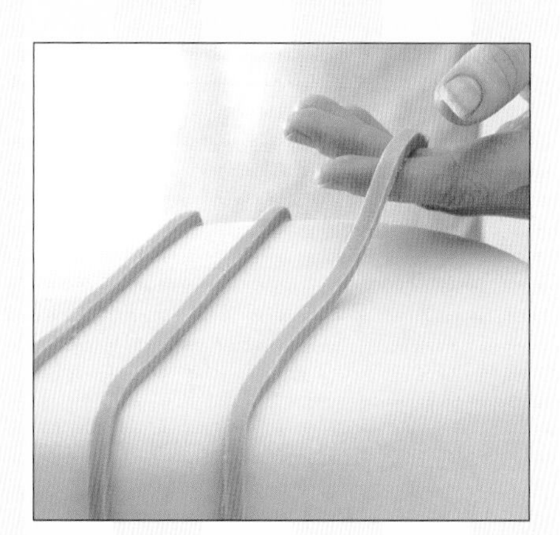

# Yule Log

**This is an excellent last-minute cake for Christmas. The jelly roll can be made with any of the suggested flavors – chocolate is traditional but often just a bit too rich for some – a whole-wheat sponge cake with nuts added makes a change. Make the sponge cake well in advance if you like, fill it with buttercream and freeze. Allow an hour for the cake to defrost before decorating.**

**Serves 8**

- 3-egg Jelly Roll (page 17) made with whole-wheat flour
- 1/4 cup flaked almonds (or chopped mixed nuts)
- 1 quantity Buttercream (page 23)
- 4-6 squares bitter chocolate
- 1tbsp unsweetened cocoa powder
- a little sifted confectioners' sugar
- 1-2tsp boiled water

1 Make and bake the jelly roll, adding the flaked almonds with the flour. Roll up, cool, and un-roll. Then fill with half the buttercream and re-roll.

2 Melt the chocolate until smooth. Spread out in two or more batches on trays, a marble board, or a clean work surface, and flatten it evenly with a spatula. If your kitchen is warm, spread the chocolate on trays that can be moved to a cooler place.

3 Allow the chocolate to cool until it loses its shine. Keep testing the edges to check for setting so it does not cool too much and set hard. When it has set too much you will have to melt it again.

4 Use a clean paint stripper or wide metal spatula to push through the chocolate, making thick curls or cigar-type rolls, or thinner curls if you prefer. Put the curls in a cool place until required.

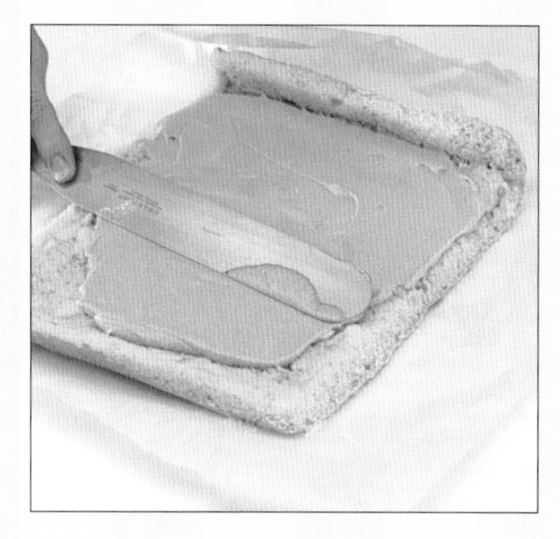

5 Blend the cocoa powder with the water and then beat this into the remaining buttercream. Beat well until really smooth, then spread thinly and evenly all over the jelly roll.

6 Immediately arrange the chocolate curls neatly all over the cake to resemble a pile of logs. Dust with a little confectioners' sugar if you wish and keep in a cool place until ready to serve.

# Happiness and Harmony Wedding Cake

**Serves 20-30**

9in square Dark Rich Fruit Cake (page 20)
Apricot Glaze (page 26)
1 1/2 lb Marzipan (page 26)
1 1/2 lb Royal Icing (page 28)
cream edible food coloring (or mix tiny amounts of sunflower, chestnut and tangerine)
snowflake sparkle dust
bright pink carnations and greenery
gold and bright pink ribbons
11in square board

**The decoration on this cake is influenced by feng shui. The intertwined fishes represent harmony and peace, while fresh flowers add a splash of color.**

1 Brush the cake with apricot glaze and cover with marzipan. Coat with pale ivory cream colored royal icing. Lightly ice the board. When all icing is dry, fix the cake in place on the board with royal icing.

2 Use the small template (page 96) to make four pairs of run-out fish in white royal icing and leave to set. When completely dry, dust with snowflake sparkle. Attach a gold ribbon and a thinner pink ribbon around the base of the cake.

3 Mark the top and sides in half, into triangles. With a no.1 nozzle, pipe fine snail piping along the base of the cake and up the sides at the corners. Outline the upper triangle with snail or zig-zag piping. Fill the triangle with cornelli piping (page 36).

4 Outline each triangle on the top of the cake with snail or zig-zag piping. Mark and pipe a large fish run-out directly onto the cake using the larger template (page 96). Fill in the second triangle with cornelli piping. Leave to dry.

5 Attach the small fish to the sides with royal icing. Leave to set thoroughly, then dust with a little more snowflake sparkle. Attach fresh flowers at the last moment.

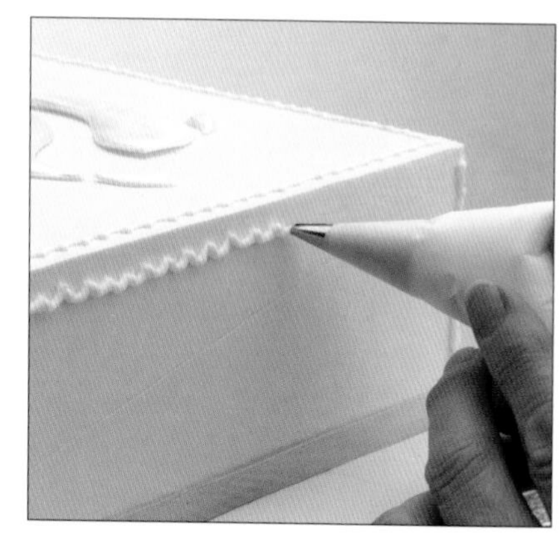

# Love Birds Wedding Cake

**Stunning birds in white and bronze make the perfect wedding cake top piece. Clever cutters are used to make the dove shapes and surprisingly simple piping with dramatic use of ribbons and bows completes the decoration.**

**Serves 100**

6in, 8in, and 12in round Dark Rich Fruit Cakes (page 20)
Apricot Glaze (page 26)
$2^1/_2$lb Marzipan (page 26)
$2^1/_2$lb Sugar Paste (page 30)
$^1/_2$lb pastillage or flower paste mix
$^1/_2$lb Royal Icing (page 28)
apricot or skin-tone edible food color
copper and white satin lustre dust powders
dove patchwork cutters
Gildesol edible gilding medium
edible glue
floristry wire
white tape
bronze, apricot, and white ribbons
14in round cake board

1 Brush all three cakes with apricot glaze and cover with marzipan. Cover them with varying shades of apricot sugar paste. Leave to firm up. Cover at least 2in of the edge of the cake board with sugar paste and frill it with a fine toothpick or frilling tool.

2 Prepare the pastillage according to the packet instructions. Roll it out very thinly and cut out as many doves as possible – they are very fragile so it is a good idea to allow for breakages. Follow the instructions with the dove cutters to get good shape definition. Use a paintbrush to carefully remove the shapes from the cutters.

3 Cover wires with white tape and then carefully attach them to the backs of the doves with glue. Leave to set for several hours. Brush half the dove shapes with Gildesol and then brush with bronze satin dust. Brush the remaining dove shapes with Gildesol and white dust. Leave to set for several hours.

4 Cut a piece of fine graph paper long enough to go around the largest cake. Place this around the cake. Pin prick fine marks as a guide for the top and bottom of each line of dots. Mark the sides of the other cakes in the same way. Then pipe fine dots in rows around the sides of all three cakes. Leave to set.

5 Trim the edges of the cakes and the base board with bronze ribbon. Make two or three large ribbon bows and attach them to pieces of covered floristry wire.

6 Place the cakes on top of each other, set back, not centered. Very carefully place a bow on each side of the assembled cakes. Place two, four, or more doves facing each other on the top cake. Add extra doves with the bows on either side of the lower tiers if you wish.

**Making Favors**

To make favors, wrap apricot and bronzed sugared almonds in fine white netting and tie with very fine ribbon. To bronze the almonds, brush with Gildesol and bronze dust.

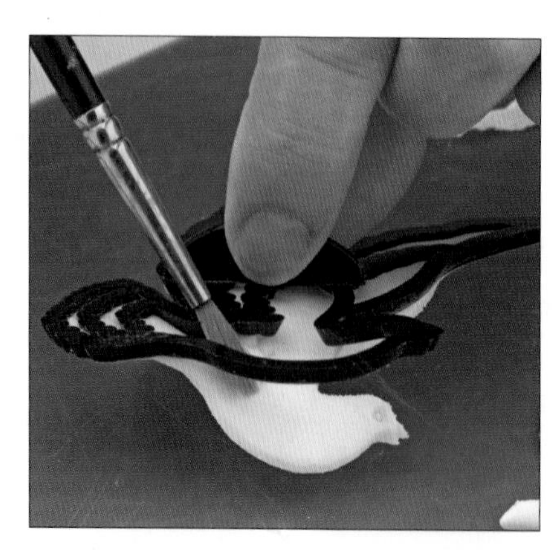

# Templates

**Petal Power Cake** (page 68)
Enlarge to 200% size for
8in cake
**Piped Chocolate Decoration**
(page 43)
**Cup Cakes** (page 48)
**Butterfly Thank You Cake**
(page 70)
**Simple Decoration for**
**Sponge Cake** (page 18)
Enlarge to 200% size
for 8in cake
**Happiness and Harmony**
**Wedding Cake**
(page 92)